Praise for Robert Kelly

"Wake up / Write down," a brief fragment—a mantra, in fact—from a recent work by Robert Kelly, I take as core insight into Kelly's poetic processes. These dailynesses, diastoles & systoles, in- & ex-pirations, create the tidal ebb & flow of outside & inside, of world & word that give rise to poetry. An alchemy that isn't about making gold, but that creates light—so as better to also see the shadows—for our hearts & minds. Or as Kelly puts it early on in this excellent new gathering: "Ox. House. Camel. / Door. Window. . . . The alphabet holds us together / pebble by pebble." **—PIERRE JORIS**

May it be said that Robert Kelly has written one of the greatest bodies of poetry in English? Not in that outdated, top-of-the-pinnacle sense, for we know now that poetry has many streams and many collectives of readers, but in the perennial sense of great even greatest. Not for the magnitude of the 90-plus books of poetry and prose and not because the work has engaged with 20th and 21st century experimentation with form and probably all poetic traditions, for that is how Robert Kelly's poetries have manifested; as a propulsive language formation finding every which way to say, to find out. His body of work is singular because of the various, particular and omnidirectional vision it offers us of how it is to be a human on earth. No other poetry realizes the elusive sacred with such breadth and depth of language, imaginally aligned with, inside of, and twined among, our shabby, fantastic existences, as in: ". . . here has here in it, / here is right here, underfoot, / my hand in your hand, here / has no glamor, only the magic of being." **—KIMBERLY LYONS**

LINDEN WORD
ROBERT KELLY

ISBN: 978-0-9997028-8-8

BSE Books are distributed by
Small Press Distribution
 1341 Seventh Street
 Berkeley, CA 94710
 orders@spdbooks.org | www.spdbooks.org
 1-800-869-7553

BSE Books can also be purchased at
www.blacksquareeditions.org and www.hyperallergic.com

Contributions to BSE can be made to
 Off the Park Press, Inc.
 976 Kensington Ave.
 Plainfield, NJ 07060
 (Please make checks payable to Off the Park Press, Inc.)

To contact the Press please write:
 Black Square Editions
 1200 Broadway, Suite 3C
 New York, NY 10001

An independent subsidiary of Off the Park Press, Inc.
Member of CLMP.

Publisher: John Yau
Editors: Ronna Lebo and Boni Joi
Design & composition: Shanna Compton

Cover art: Sylvia Plimack Mangold, *The Linden Trees with Blue Glaze*,
1989. Oil on linen,.40 1/8 x 30 in. (102 x 76 cm). Courtesy Alexander
and Bonin, New York.

So much of this is
from,
so all of this is
for,
Charlotte

Contents

Foreword

This book reflects a year or so of concentration on the poem as structure, poem as house. Stanza is the key, it means *room* in Italian, each stanza different in shape and function, like the rooms of a house—every room in the house is, must be, different—the kitchen is not the bedroom. So stanzas serve varied functions, welcome differing guests of meaning and music.

RK, Autumn 2022

Elements of Calculus

The pebbles on Church's Beach
all point across the bay
to the mainland, America,
insofar as round things
can point anywhere. Mostly
round. Worn by tide, time,
friction, glacial enterprise,
all the usual suspects. Last night
I learned how to unwrap
cough drops from their twisted
paper. Paper is supposed to be
just for writing on. Cellophane
was made for secular occasions,
paper for sacred. Writing
manifestos, wiping the body,
dabbing tears from lovers' eyes,
all the holy things. The beauty
of pebbles is they do all our
counting for us–no numbers needed,
the beach accepts the sea.
The vacant lot across the street
possessed a deep declivity
as if an old foundation planned,
just deep enough for us
on snowy days to sled down
not far but fun, micro-alpine
pleasures in the city, or more

truly towards the city's edge–
we had the last candy store
before the marshes on the sea.
The way pebbles roll.
This is the enactment of the play
the characters asleep in the script,
the actors relaxing in the room
they call Eden, innocence and wine
until cast out into the next act
and whoever they are vanishes
into whomever they must be.
Become. Please keep listening.
You hear the pebbles rolling
down the sidewalk, one of them
caught in your sneaker, digit
on a digit, don't count, get it out–
you are suzerain of your shoes.
Banish interlopers, those numbers
from the banker's bench, those
guesstimates of lethal sciences,
silence, look at the sea.
That's Massachusetts over there
and Rhode Island in your left hand,
life of danger, merry-go-round
in Rockaway, hear the music,
calliope knows best, rub two
between your palms, pebbles,
and feel the rhythm of creation–
do we create what we behold?

The bus stops across the street,
the subway five blocks away,
see what life is like?
We are children of the distances,
no mama but the waking light,
day is here, go do it all again.
Stone by stone it signifies.
But you have to read it—that's
the hard part. Here, let me
show you how. Ox. House. Camel.
Door. Window. Man asleep
on a blanket on the floor.
The alphabet holds us together
pebble by pebble. As many
as it takes to fill up a figure
irregular in shape, a hip or a
hummock on a hillslope, how
can we measure the inner
meanings of what we see?
We see curved space with straight
line eyes—that is our religion
from the start, Karahan, Jerusalem.
Hold firm, a generous hand often
has gaps between the fingers—
through those pebbles tend to fall
you end up with fewer stones now
than you thought, but did you ever
count them? Not then, not now,
it's still New Bedford over there,

the best ice cream on Ile-St-Louis,
pebbles, always more pebbles
until the mind is done. Exalted
over the plain, smiling like lavender
on the slopes by Cavaillon, river
after river until the word is said.
Even then it's hard to hear—
imagine Aeneas trudging upstream
on foot for once, boat and sea
far behind him, us I mean, imagine
the long walk to get where we are.
Aren't we refugees from a lost city,
pebbles in our pockets, there must
be a place up ahead, place for us,
stones too yearn to come home.

Discomforts of Arithmetic

Those chilly gaps
between the numerals,
water from the fountain
slipping through your fingers.

How many are there? How many
is water? How many is air?
I smelled your hair
when you bent close, intent
on some other number.

How much am I, how many?
I said to the tree Come sleep in me
but they're busy now, trying
to forget each leaf they had
to make next year's even better.

And they count each one. The way
we blink our eyes, constantly
renewing the seen. The scene.
The word meant shadow long ago—
who dares count so many years?

Someone not long ago has proved
there are no random numbers.
So pick a number and somehow it
is already yours, has chosen you,
as air slips between collar and skin,

always trying to come closer.
Do numbers have a home, perhaps
in us, they yearn for and hurry
to reach or to approximate, as we
guess how fast our car is going

by how fast the trees pass by?
Does everything have a number too
or is it just us, refugees from Eden
where there was only one. Until
a furtive computation came along.

1 January 2022

Aquila

Spread of eagle wings
over the river now,
we see them there,
famous whitehead American bird,
shadow of empery aloft
sailing low sometimes
just over the bridge.

2.

O the shadow of things
she cried, as one fell
across her lap,
looked up and it was gone.

3.

Things anticipate their shadows.
I am this so that I can be that.
History is made of horrors cast
by sudden surges of energy,
wingflaps of will and want.

4.

But eagles on the estuary
seem purer than that.

Slow patrol, big, big
and we like big. But Ben
Franklin thought the turkey
should be the nation's bird,
big enough and lots of them,
good to eat and they
shit all over the place
nourishing the earth
we live on, seldom
bothering the empty sky.

2 January 2022

In Leviticus
you read the code,
it speaks language
no one made
or all humans did
fast asleep in the desert
then woke up speaking.
We're still trying
to make sense of what we said.

2.

Colder today,
the mist is less.
Sometimes weather helps,
sometimes a bird hops by
interested in what it finds on earth.
So much to learn!
All life a crowded schoolroom,
read the maxims hung on the wall.

3.

Casuists. Jesuits. Sanhedrin.
We do these things to ourselves,
complex situations here
bear fake solutions forged there,
back then, deep in the forget.

4.

"We live nearby so we can be friends."
The simplicity of what got said,
rich polyphony of a single Yes.

5.

So the code can be
as they say broken
and the juice pour out,
pomegranate to begin with
so many crystals to make one.
And then the scent of lavender
and after long centuries the rose.

2 January 2022

The Spanish Armada comes every night,
we find its wreckage on the beach at dawn,
our swans peck cautiously
at oranges from Màlaga
bobbing on the surf. Flotsam.
Then daylight too washes up on shore,
we wake with our own wings
thick and torpid at our sides.

2.

All day we try to reclaim images,
merchandise of dream,
slippery with oil the Arabs
taught Spain to grow and press and pour,
cannon balls and grappling hooks,
torches flung, sails on fire,
seagulls diving, swimmers reach the sand,
lie there looking at the blue sky,
a schoolboy goes by chanting Latin.

3 January 2022

Nomina Numina

Names woke me,
litany of aunts and uncles,
sunshine, somebody's rabbit.

2.

What to do with a day
that has no name
or only one left over
from last week, next week,
ancient gods of war?
The French kept a calendar a while
where every day of the year
had its own name,
but had to share that name
with some plant or tree or tool,
nothing of its only own.

3.

We say Today
and hope that counts,
sun in the trees at last
after a week of mist.
And this poor dear new year
has only a number not a name,
but you have a name

and I have one too
yet even so we all
sleep in the bosom of Now.

4 January 2022

Together

As close as we came
there were still miles
inside that got not said.
Awkward pressed together
in this closet that knows
how to walk down the street.
Dour within, we sense
it skip kid-like through trash,
those solid shadows of desire
we too know all too much about.

2.

Close? There are religions
further than that.
Love you said is a spiel
from a con man but what
we have is truer than that—
true because there is no
word that says it, no word
at all. But I could hear it.

3.

So a bridge does go there,
almost every city has its bridges

if only to get out of town.
I saw Golden Gate at sunset
so close they seemed married.
But in that city no one is.

4.

Heavy traffic of the heart.
So close we thought together,
no bridge between, the cables
by which we are suspended
welded to the highest ideals.
At three we learned to read,
the pages are still turning.

5.

Close. Closer than I've ever been,
sometimes I forget which side
of the bed my legs are on. Love
whatever else it does approximates
and its deep trust can be a burden
on the trusted beloved. Otherwise
we'd all be in love all the time
and Dante would have nothing
but Hell to write about, but all
the birds would learn to sing.
But who would listen? Love,

be close enough to hear the silence
that thrills us in the empty room,
thresholds everywhere, we dare
to enter, hoping to find us there.

5 January 2022

How Many Suns

to make this day?
Snow covered,
bright in a blue way,
why are colors
anyhow? Every day
a mystery, every prayer
begs for information.

2.

Homework of the river,
the spotted lens.
Clean the land,
we feed the sea.

3.

A girl in gingham
is an oracle,
a man in overalls
adjusts the orb.
Hidden constellations
revealed only when
you dare to lie on your side.

4.

Piecemeal, like scripture,
thousands of little words
to make word. Snowflakes
last five thousand years.

5.

The lost tribes of Israel
gather in my living room.
They teach me Gaelic,
I feed them fresh coffee.
Everything comes from Africa.

6.

And then the dream began—
intelligent men around me,
fraternal, good-humored,
saying wise things. Forget
the message, remember the feel.

7.

Snow script
dense tangled branches.
We see only
what we are prepared to see.

8.

Even inside gloves
the hands are cold.
In the brightest room
shadows lurk.
It seems I try
to keep myself afraid,
as if fear were the best
protection against what I fear.

9.

Ghosts before breakfast
like Hans Richter's film,
night's fingers leave smudges,
no phone rings.
It's all out there,
waking world,
dogs on leashes,
the broken chain.
Try hard, so hard,
to accept the neutrality of noon.

10.

Sometimes it's all right there.
You don't have to think.
Other times

be a good neighbor
to your thoughts,
let them play in your yard,
put up with their loud music.
They are your only local friends.

7 January 2022

Night-Blooming Jasmines of Montreux

How many years it's bloomed
since H.D. stood near the shore
and breathed their meaning in.
It smelled like time to her,
time, the animal from which
all poetry and narrative are born,
song is time that we can hear
it tells us what we're thinking.

Not so many years ago we stood
in front of that hotel, breathing in
that amazing sensuous odor
for ourselves, and tried to name
the darker shapes in France
across the lake, we could see
the peak above St Jean far inland,
the lights of Evian, Thonon, no
late ferry bothering the lake.

Scent of the flowers, shapes
of night-time distances, all poetry
is made of distance, one heart
to another, every word's meaning
locked inside the hearer's thought.
So close we stood together, lake
and flowers, man and woman,
and the distances always win.

21 January 2022

Coastlines

Along the coast
stratifications of what
can still be known
and the rifts, gaps, caves
where feeling haunts
the habit of our seeing.

2.

Even I have been there.
Red sands of the Hadramaut
endlessly everywhere void
as Ozymandias then suddenly
a highway and a little car,
just like reality.

3.

Or further red, the quiet
mountains of Anatolia,
look down, own eyes,
that's what traveling is for,
not getting somewhere,
there is nowhere we have to be.

4.

But I bless the anticline
of this country here
that is sort of mine,
to gaze, even passing fast,
at that rock is to sense
an obligation, to pay attention,
be responsible to each stratum,
to be able to respond
to each compressed layer of
all that happened.

5.

Is it enough to let it dream in us?
Something has to be said.
Something always has to be said.
The coast is continuous,
No way for it to stop.
The length of the coastline
in relation to the area of the land
enclosed determines
the political impact of the island.
Work it out. Call it the Greece.
And politics is everything we do.
The rock keeps us writing.

23 January 2022

Signs

The word went out
to see for itself,
don't ask me why,
all I can do is follow it
down the Orinoco or
Kentucky caves or where
would you go? Names
of places bring me home,
one degree warmer than
an hour before, yet I dreamt
other people's dreams
and lost my own.

2.

Morning does that, the old
stupid potent question,
am I who I was?
And if not, where has he gone?
that mindset that was me,
now out in elsewhere,
maybe following the word?

3.

The first year
it iced up here

a fellow drove
his blue sedan
across the frozen
Hudson all the way
to Saugerties and back.
Fact. I didn't see it
but I can see it still.
He was Irish I think,
I hope he still is.

4.

The Buddhist teacher
rewrote Descartes: *Cogito
ergo non adsum*. I think,
therefore I am not present.
A lovely thing about a word:
it does your thinking for you
leaves you free
to be, right here,
maybe even now,
while it goes searching,
researching, remembering.

5.

We lived near an airfield
and a zeppelin came by,
lived near the ocean

and some of me still does.
Zeppelins are over now
but the ocean still smiles.
That's about all I've learned.

6.

The little I can do
is never enough,
is always enough.

Yesterday you saw
a robin, heard
a Carolina wren.

Whatever happens
is enough to go on.
For example, the sky.

7 January 2022

It had to begin somewhere,
the line wound tight around his chest,
"my lungs are a sewing machine,
god knows where the cloth comes from
it keeps stitching, speaking,
spilling out of me into,
I don't know, where does it go?"
But knowing had nothing to do with it,
knowing is a soft organ
in hard bone, "my thoughts
are fossils of what had been me,"
but that was thinking,
thinking has nothing to do
till it's all done.
And it was only beginning,
if even that, what
was his breath up to now?
Some days are bright
even when you can't see the Sun.

2.

The line kept getting tighter,
slowly, so slim, not like the rope
sailors call line, lean, lean,
like a quick definition
in a cheap dictionary,

tree, a wooden thing with leaves.
But still it kept pressing in,
sometimes he was afraid
it would cut right through,
skin and bone and all
and leave him cut in two,
and even then his parts
would not be symmetrical,
brain and breath, but all the rest
flotsam sailors mock from deck,
"why am I thinking about the sea,
is it to avoid thinking about me?
Are we the same? Is anybody there,
drunken sailors, sober priests?"

3.

Of course no answer came.
No answer comes.
An answer is right there all along,
like April's leaf in January's tree.
Speaking of speaking,
he closed his eyes.

4.

There was no pain as such.
Maybe the line has loosened
as he had slept, dozed a dozen breaths

as his grandmother used to say,
looking at her husband by the hearth,
prayer book open on his blanketed lap.
Short sleeps are the dreamiest of all,
"but why am I dreaming,
or even sleeping?
There is so much work to be done,
something begun."

5.

He listened for the sound of water,
water always knows,
toilet flush or hurricane,
listen hard, what it says comes fast.
"I have stuffed my ears with music
so I did not have to hear
what everything was saying.
And yet in music I heard
something breathe, just
outside the door, sometimes
I opened it fast to let it in
and now the line plays out
around me, waiting to begin."

6.

He could use a ladder if he rose,
could climb and let the line dangle,

dangle down to touch the ground—
when it reached earth he'd know
he'd climbed as far as he had to go.
Then where would he be?
At some woman's window?
Leaf-choked gutter on his own old house,
maybe even at the top of the wall?
A comfortable feeling filled him,
family dinner? end of the opera?
at the sense of looking
at last over the wall.

7.

But it wasn't
and he didn't,
it was just more thinking.
But the line laxed a bit,
he lazed his way into the day,
forgetting all the dream stuff
or whatever it was,
night's menu, filled with unknown offerings.
His lungs even relaxed,
a glimpse of breath
and then it was day.

28 January 2022

Towards the Great House

Caster under furniture
moves the world round,
this house, Charles,
this memory place,
or is it palace after all
and we after all
a little wiser?

2.

Be ordinary
for Christ's sake,
he walked among us,
all we need is road,
the firm re-spelling of geography.
Walk, because it's hard.

3.

But you didn't care about the money,
you showed me the check
you wouldn't cash,
just gave enough cash
to buy a potato in winter,
like now, blizzard up the coast,
pray it veers out to sea.

4.

Right here wind
puffs snow off the roof
fast, like a kid's first cigarette.
We smoked in those days,
people did a lot of things
and things did them right back.

5.

O the town you cared so deeply for,
I have no town of my own,
and your town was not just the actual
but all the possible cities
energy and brain could constellate,
let's shake hands on it,
we need a new city,
we've been waiting out here too long,
at half-imaginary addresses,
a new city, grid and beach,
never mind the showy towers,
they always got us into trouble,
cling to contour, stay close to water,
leave the sky to the birds.

6.

We need a house
for all our houses

to live in,
just as we went
from cave to stone to wood
so our houses must
glass or brick of metal
have a great house of their own,
dome of pure energy
over our city
to leave the weather out there
and turn our labors
only to the weather of heart's mind
build it, savants,
forget the Moon,
forget probing the remote
while our lives are at the mercy
of what happens here.
Project that spacious dome
of pure energy over us,
let us be everything that happens.

29 January 2022

1.

Time is a step
on another road.
Where does it go with us—
we linger to find out.
Wayside comforts,
filling stations for the weary heart,
all the lucent maybes
glittering like garnet
pebbles on the rock slope.
And we climb.

2.

This is serious, this
is human manners,
broadcloth costumes,
eyelashes, flower petals,
passports, wedding rings.

3.

The black bishop of Newark
gave me my charge:
Open the door and keep on
opening it. The yellow

Lama of Nangchen
gave me all the language
to do it with. The white
mother who bore me
gave me my hands.
That's all I know about color.

4.

Forgive the shift in register,
it gets personal sometimes
between the rocks,
snow humps in the mogul
we swivel to descend
faster than our brethren
to the sentence's end.
I saw them on television
and could hear what the snow said.
Weather is laughing at us anyhow.

5.

Back to time, our master.
Sunday morning, 18 degrees.
Yes, I've noticed, this sermon
made up of names and numbers
and no thing we dare touch.
Remember Thomas Wolfe
who lived just down the river,

dahin, dahin! he cried out
in German, away, away, so far away,
guessing where time takes
anything that matters.

6 February 2022

Can it be the other way,
the other side of the street at last
where some girl lives
you'll never know
but you walk on her sidewalk
watching a sparrow
making some use of a bare tree,
yes, you think, it could be me.
Because that is what music is
and does, *the shadow follows
wherever I go*, you know that too.
You know what the priest says
not a matter of getting what you
want but wanting what you get.
That's what streets are for.

9 February 2022

1.

The inchoate miracle
begins. By noon
it will be now.

2.

Scattered in the gravel
old carnelians
engraved with faces,
emperors and saints,
we have little
more than words to guide us.

3.

So we anticipate the past.
Was Gesar really Caesar?
Did only one thing ever happen
and it's not finished yet?

4.

Boys should stay out of history,
they have a slippery sense of fact.
Leave the chronicle to women

who know the order of things,
who know the difference.

5.

That sounds severe
but was a cry for help,
man floundering in the surf,
the names, the names,
the tall oak trees of Dodona.

12 February 2022

Be in no body
the print-out read,
small print, fuzzy—
as if today the body
is what we must come out of,
not go further in,
our own or someone's else,
somebody as we say.

2.

The words said not be in
but did not specify go out.
Is there that other place,
fabulous queendom of Between,
where all the body knows
meets the live knowing
of the other?

3.

Maybe the dream tonight
will clarify what last
night's edict proclaimed.
Maybe along the way
I'll find out what being means.

12 February 2022

Coast

The sand was red—
that much was obvious
even to me. A mile or two
of Flagler Beach empty for spring.
For me and thee and pelican,
just like alchemy.
And I was healed,
emblems of my craft
renewed. And the sea
granted me fellowship
and I could bring
my true self home.

15 February 2022

Kinderszenen

Making problems
out of solutions,
children are good at that,
little alchemists with
knotted brow,

                              don't

squint so hard, the right
answer opens a dark door.

2.

You know how the cellar is,
OK in daylight when the sun
filters in through the peach tree
and the fuzzy window screen.
But come the dark run
up the creaky stairs—
ascend! Moab is up there,
Nebo, Everest, at least
the sofa of Paradise.

3.

I know whereof it speaks,
I too in a made-over coal bin
brought the clunky machinery
of being me, chemicals, radio,

typewriter, table, chair. There,
a place to work it out.
And every answer
makes the problem worse.

4.

Not evil, just hard to deal with.
What do you do with a word
once you've said it? And when
the solution turns blue in the tube,
what on this blossoming earth
do you do with what you know?

5.

Because it really is springtime,
even down there, here,
cold dark, switch off the desk lamp,
sit in the quiet, maybe a mouse,
maybe the wind in the bushes,
maybe the enigma of silence.

6.

You've spent so many years
here, in childhood, working it out,
sighing, going up to bed,
dreaming about Mary

fleeing Jerusalem, on her way
to Glastonbury. Didn't
you meet Them there
not so many years ago?

17 February 2022

A Long Line Running from Aldebaran

ends in a sparkle on our aventurine,
ring on finger, song on lips,
the human hum vibrates through space
and answers the stars, epic
consequences discovered
almost entirely in dream.
Or in your native rock.
Terminal moraine, glacial plain,
your glorious pale yellow sand.

2.

Stand at the mirror
and repeat after me,
always do what glass
tells you to do.
Because glass was sand once
and sand is rock, close enough
to diamond to pay all your bills,
the rent you pay to live
in a spacious language
with heat and running water.

3.

Epic, I said, the long song
of how everything happened

after the prose of how it all began.
How long it took to give
names to all the stars we could see
not we, they, the ones who loved
out on the sands where night is clean,
not the mists of our wet skies.
But here we see them too,
from time to time, their Arab names
twinkling in our books,
and that river that reminded
us poor children of our spilled milk.
But how long it took
the light to reach your finger,
white sapphire today,
more costly, stone of Venus—
while usually her eyes are blue
love makes the light true.

4.

So where did love come in?
Not in Homer, not much in Olson
but we fools find it under every stone.
Pick one up with me. Toss
history away, skim it on the pond, one two even three
skips before it sinks, toss
it in the sea, the soft hollow
left in the earth is what it means,

this love stuff, this yielding
into one another when the war is done.

5.

I was never good at throwing things away,
my mind cluttered with rich randomness,
I could never skip stones the way
my father could,
I could pitch a mean curve
but what good is that
when no one's at bat,
wait, wait, there's a song
in this, yes, a star
is a southpaw in the sky
and we are all at bat.
Use the stone to catch
the truth of what it launches,
even though the song now peters out.

6.

But the names we give Up There,
the Ghoul, the Dog, but pretty
Cassiopeia combing her long hair,
who knew, who told, who went
up there and came back down
smug with secret knowing?

The line reaches down to us
stretches through us, points
if we follow it to that unimaginable
place beyond names
when we have spoken all the names
and used up all the words.

21 February 2022

Cavernous, the thought of you
walking through my mind
the way you do, the way they do
once you know them and are known.
All my corridors you know
better than I do, the little windows
that let the least light in,
you find your way.
Tell me what you find.
Tell me where I am,
hollow earth theory of the heart.

1 March 2022

Doves

Doves flutter in a cautious rose bush,
crow perches on a steeple—
which is truer?
                          What kind of people
worship in a stone chapel,
stone house, trying to understand
what the stone remembers?
O brick is made of bread and water,
a leaf is made from rain and laughter
all leaves are tongues, they tell
what the wind and earth tell them,
raise a glass to a stranger's window,
wet with rain, engrailed with vines
leaves tell the grapes all they know
and the wine remembers.
Lick the glass to taste the final truth.

3 March 2022

I Write to You in Thinglish

because I know no other way,
a hand, a knee, a sheet
of paper, a rose petal
found in the snow outside
a florist's door, a blue car
goes by when all the cars
are black and grey and white,
a fox in the backyard, yes,
feed him too, a book on the table,
don't even have to open it,
enough that it's there,
enough that it's there.

5 May 2022

She had learned too much down there to be let back on earth, especially with a husband who poured out songs and secrets the way a barmaid gushes wine from her pitcher. No, she had to pretend to die again slid back down the long muddy chute into Uncle Hades' estate, where she, and what she knew, would be safe. Of course they would let her tell, tell true, bit by bit, year by year, to those of her husband's tribe who cared to, dared to, listen to her whispers, rising right from the underworld into the ear inside the ear.

12 March 2022

The Ides of March

The odes warned us:
passions are knives
we might be slain
in the senate house
of our thoughts,
velleities, feelings. Beware.

2.

But we thought it was just history,
we did not recognize
that I am Caesar, every one of me,
and Brutus (*kai su, tekne*)
my fondest thought.

3.

Wounded by desire
we stumble to many strange altars,
kneel there, growl or whimper,
not sure to whom we pray,
is that Venus or Minerva,
or my own twisted shadow
on the old tile wall?

4.

History is only you.
You are the rebel
and the murdered king,
the prophet risen
and the prophet slain,
the senate and the thousand
campfires of an army on the plain.
No one but you, the other name of me.

15 March 2022

The flower of being where she is
scents the whole day with color.
She walks alone along her river.
She understands.

2.

Sometimes, staring at the church
spring up from the far shore
she feels she is a word, a new
word about to be spoken.

3.

Her mother told her so many things
but this thing she left for her
to discover herself. In herself.
Feel of her tongue on the roof of her mouth
all over her body, making sense.

4.

The river was a part of the equation,
like the equals-sign pointing
to the x she aimed at.
Flow me with thee
she felt herself saying
and the language too was new.

5.

All the way, all the way,
that's all she demanded
of herself or of that other
self, the city around her
pierced by the river.
She looked over at the church again
and thought the body reaches
to the end of the soul,
and wondered if it was permitted
to think that thought.
Or any thought. Who are you,
she begged, Who are you?

17 March 2022

Pebbles

I counted the pebbles
counted them again,
different sum, different stones,
even the fingers
were not the same.

                              Dreams do that
and not just dreams.

2.

Trees are waking now,
we'll be less lonely.
We'll all take our proper pills
and imagine morning.
Think: Light is a gift
we give to one another.
Every day is Christmas morning.
Don't be so silly. Why not?
Silly used to mean holy—
how do we get holy now?

3.

Encumbered with the obvious
we slack towards sleep.
A week ago we could have sledded
but the snow has melted now

and birds are many,
speaking of holy, messengers
busy in our seed—
I cherish the ambiguity.

4.

Empson called it amphibolity,
saying two things at once
and meaning them. I deem
most every word amphibolous—
think of what you mean by me.
And tree always stands for something else.

5.

Close the word book, baby,
and use the words,
scribble them in lipstick
on urgent surfaces
until even we can get the message
if there is one. Ask the birds.

20 March 2022

Needs

Taste of what I need,
handful of other,
a stroll on the cliff
high above now.
Somewhere down there
I am waiting to begin.

2.

That's everyday stuff,
the spice of light, gloom
of empty hands. Hurry,
hurry is its own reward.

3.

It is indeed somewhat
like an opera. Grass,
car, road, tree. Birds.
How can it end? You bring
your own music to the theater
and the town does all the rest.

4.

By town we mean the place
surrounded, the fenced-in real,

the glorious ordinary. Big
as you like or little hillside,
a town, a tune, go
limp around its waltz.

5.

The color's all gone
into that little blue bottle again
windowsill of a grey day.
Weather's best when you hardly
notice it, someone's hand
lightly on your knee.

6.

Look, someone walking up the road!
By the time I write it down
the figure's gone. Man or woman
who can tell now, the word stays,
the flesh is gone.

7.

But that's what color does,
leads to metaphysics
surely as your grandmother
led you to the wishing well
and made you look therein
to see what or who was

doing all that wishing.
A color is your self come home.

8.

Hence all the fuss about grey
and green and slide trombones
yelping through the long parade,
because noises have colors too,
you don't need Rimbaud
to tell you that, though he gave you
so much of what you really need.

9.

Participate. Be
the color the world needs
right now, be sure
you're the right one,
measure the music,
pull the shimmer round you,
dance the seven veils
of the spectrum one by one
on the body till the day is born.

10.

I apologize for one more
cultural reference, So hard
to get away from what one thinks.

11.

So when I came in last night
I thought you were playing the flute
or the penny-whistle in a distant room
the way you used to play
The *Lament for Limerick*
till even my eyes paid their tribute
to it, to you, not to the losses
but all that music finds.
It was some other sound
but you were there, are here,
slowly colors are coming back.

23 March 2022

Glass

1.

Glance at the mirror
nobody there,
a whole day off,
free of being,
of being me.

2.

So what should who
do with this free day,
kiss the spring wind,
prat to the tree?

3.

Write trilogy
about going upstairs,
or with a chunk of blue chalk
draw a dolphin on a rock
and watch some ocean come to it.

4.

It's not so easy to begin
so don't decide.
Look up and watch what

your hands are doing
up in the air, signaling?
waving to the empty tower,
or are you flying?

5.

Not so sure about that mirror,
a sheen of winter still in the glass.
Maybe not as awake as one needs
to be to be. Maybe look again,
tired eyes, the script of years?

6.

No, no, he cried,
for I am new,
this day is never
and always,
sugar and spice
and a bird on the tree
singing so sweet
Don't Listen To Me.

7.

I was that wing once
and you were the other,
remember how we flew
to all the nowheres-in-particular

where birds are most at home,
even those grey forests where
trees have roofs and windows.
Watch the people—one day
we will be them too.

8.

But happy enough being here
when the wound doesn't hurt
and the air is calm.
Nothing wrong
with as we are.
Or is that just one more religion?

9.

Read the book and find out—
anything's a bible
if you take its word for it.
Its Book of Revelation
is an empty page.

10.

Does that mean Go
back to bed some more
and sleep my way to hope?
Children in the sacristy
yearning to be acolytes—

serve the Service, sustain
the tottering old priest.

11.

You call that a dream?
I'd call it a harmless spider
crawling on your wrist
where a watch should rest—
but you're too sly for time,
I mean I am. And late again.

12.

After the concert we lay on the grass
but I was all alone, still
the music hovered in me,
warming the night chill.
Beautiful and terrifying too—
music always leaves you here,
right where you so utterly are.

13.

And then the mirror spoke:
You blame me for
each empty room,
for every wrinkle
on your worried brow,
isn't there great joy

in looking at something
then looking away? Sad me,
a thing I don't know how to do.

14.

So here we dance around
while matter grieves,
matter strives to messiah
its way in us, till each
is born anew and I am you,
no difference, utterly distinct.
O listen to the thingly chant.

15.

If glass could float
the sky would smile—
know what I mean?
If music could just
stop for a minute
and listen to itself
it would shock us awake.
War is the worst thing of all.

16.

Canopy overhead
but no rain,
red carpet to the curb

but no car comes.
The doorman slumbers
on the steps. Ostiarius,
first of the minor orders,
the Porter who admits us
to the sacrament, the church,
the cave of wonders,
world echoing in my hollow head.

17.

And there I am at last
back in the mirror again.
Sigh of relief, mixed
a little bit with grief.
Who am I to dare to speak?
18.
Then magic. Presto!
the mirror is a window,
the gorgeous not-me out there
is singing, shining, fingering
our infantine neurology
until we feel. Weary
as a blackboard or fresh
as tangerine the tale goes on.
Every story runs two ways at once,
read backwards to get a glimpse of truth.

25 March 2022

The Geology of the Heart

1.

Profile of someone
you loved once, can't
name now, lost
in the strata
of indulgence,
layers of remorse.
I saw the face clearly
but who am I.

2.

Imagine a rose,
ordinary beauty
from the florist
or your aunt's garden,

imagine a rose
falls from your hands
onto a marble floor
and shatters

into a thousand crystals
you try to sweep together
can't get all of them, some
stick under your fingernails,

where is your rose now,
from the far end of the nave
you hear a voice, angry,
speaking yet another language.

3.

Coast of Oregon
mudstone cliffs
I sat with roses
watched the sea come in.
Real roses, real sea.
I find it nowadays
sometimes in the heart
if I may use the ordinary
name we use for that
which lives our lives for us.
Roses by the sea.
Come laugh at men.

4.

The profile was clear,
youthful, smiling soft.
Who are you, I asked
but my mind was quiet
as if to say Look,
don't talk, don't name
anything for once,

the shape of what you see
is imbedded in you,
this face also is your earth,
follow the contours silently.
Sometimes any answer is a lie.

26 March 2022

The Discernments

Hour after hour they.
Spooks on ladders,
tower windows. Pelf.
You knew it was coming
so it came. I knew
otherwise and so,
Certainty eludes. Picture
of money 0n the wall.
Aluminum pennies from the war,
most common metal of all,
noncommissioned officer,
flag drag in dirt. Apologies
galore. And more. The ghost
peers in every bloody window,
the dust speaks Latin, worry,
worry. My ankle hurts
but you're safe at home. Who.
Crouch closer listen tighter
till I tell. Do you hear it now?
Crocus by the door, wolfsbane later.
Sympathize. I'm only here today
tomorrow there's another officer
shouting nonsense orders.
At least try to smile, be a meadow
for Christ's sake, vast and green
and bounded only by far forest.
Everything has an horizon

no hope of never. Suck on pebble.
Walk to the store. Spit it out
in the gutter before you go in.
Hunger abated, cash safe in wallet
but what else is in the pocket,
eh? What else hides in your having?
Twist-ties snug your zucchini
in clearest plastic, we know
what's coming, o share
the aisle with me fair stranger,
parking lot rimmed with trees
a ballet class leaps under some
I swear, youthful defenders
of wingless flight, I grieve
for my slowness, aching toes,
busy ads between innings,
agriculture makes you wait,
is it spring yet outside the book,
wanderlust for other rooms.
Dative case. All for you,
my sweet, but who knows the noun?
Emphasis like rain on roof tile,
south of France, dormice
live up there and a bat flies by
disturbed by my inspection.
Luberon owns half the sky.
But I came back home
no worse for archeology,
that's not me talking, quoting

from a guide book to Venus
he found in dream, a friend,
among so many, yes, you,
you're a planet too, conjoint,
aching with desire, exhausted
from satisfying them, joyful
in other words in other words.
Venus! I thought he said Venice,
got cold feet, wouldn't trust
my life to one of those, boats
are no better than mosquitoes,
no mosquitoes in church, safe,
safe a few minutes till
the bell starts ringing and the guys
come shuffling up the aisle
singing stuff. Flee while you can,
the truth is out there,
sitting on the slipper steps.
And then you're home,
kitchen table with a decent cloth
spread on it and a loaf of bread.
Now try to find a toothy blade
to slice it with. See what I mean,
they're everywhere, the little problems
add up to a huge solution,
glory over the Adriatic, wait,
over Fort Greene Park too
and Rockaway and your backyard
or mine, remember peach trees

in December wrapped in burlap,
remember the first time you crossed
and saw your ancestral island
busy with shipping, Portsmouth,
early morning, trying to learn French,
why not, somebody has to answer me,
someday, some smiling sea marsh,
bittern and mallard, Mozart
on car radio, make it up,
whatever you do don't just remember.
Sanitary pages, escalator
up to non-fiction in Hyde Park,
ours, not yours, we're home now
trapped in one more sunbeam
on a cloudy day. Discover this.
It's coming, round as a plum,
sweet as a shadow, a color
she calls purple I call blue,
it's what religion does to you,
nothing ever tastes the same again.

Coda:

Maybe and maybe not.
Ask the lighthouse keeper
what he has seen from Gayhead,
what the Wampanoag let us glimpse,
a white cliff, big surf, vague
islands of no size. Ask

and if there is one he may tell
the confused dreams he has
after his legal marijuana suppers,
even Massachusetts makes mistakes,
I shouldn't be so ashamed
of my patternless sobriety.
And then the message broke off,
or did the instrument decide—
as so many of them do—enough,
poor human, thou hast heard
too much and never listened,
go back to the Chablais and carry
a loaf tucked under your arm
all the way home like a real man,
as if your feet could feel the road
and not just their own pain,
as if you could see the hillside
with no timidity, no wolf for miles,
and answer all her letters
for Christ's sake, or there He is again,
who led me down the cellar stairs
and gave me a quiet little dusty room
my own, where I learned how to learn
and learned that was enough.

27 March 2022

Alterity

Golden raptor, time's thief
wants to hear your hips
shape gravity, your lungs
let music out, you are
all other people, fascination
of the stone wall across the way
the girl next door, the Portugals
all of them beyond the seas,
son, listen to me, over there
is always a window, look,
look long as you like but no,
no suicide, no even crawling
down the ivy.
                              Hard as it is
to reckon, here is where it all is.
Your idiolect is animal enough—
take care of it, it grows sleek,
meaningful, sounds more like you
every day, until you can't
even remember me at all.
Then the shadows fall away
in the museums, the statues
come to life and bring you
sweet pomegranates in their white hands,
nobly nibble on what they offer
but never ask for more.

In one small room the river
runs from stone to sea,
a syncline by your sofa,
the moon your chandelier—
isn't that enough? Mahler
on the radio from Stephansdom,
don't cry, or don't cry yet,
all too soon a friend is at the door,
go let them in but not too far,
all the mothers of the world
will tell you this. As if a mother
is the only other you'll ever need.

8 March 2022

No Now Now.

The fang of then
sinks in the ankle—
pain is the past
lingering, consequence,
the bitter child.

2.

A little skin
of snow on the roof,
so little, just enough
to remind, weather
is never over, pale sheen,
more like a shadow than itself.

3.

After the obvious
the scholarly remorse.
How did it get into me?
What migrations
brought here here?
Ask, ask, and doubt the answer.

4.

She rode the city bus to school
Sutter Avenue seventy years ago

I did not see her face I don't
imagine it now. A person only
moving up the aisle. Images
must have a reason. Just like pain.

5.

Stop the ache
and start again.
The wheat field is waiting.
Yesterday we saw meadows
that sprawled out peaceful
in my mind as much as out there,
there is a joy in meadows
rising gently towards the sky.
Nobody there. So there
I send my mind and lay it down
easy in deep grass, study
the blank sky until its words
start to appear. Everything
knows how to write.
The pain is almost gone.

28 March 2022

The Book I Want to Read

is hidden on your shelf.
I want to leaf through it,
let my fingers feel
the pages as they ripple past,
I want to feel the words
rough and smooth long
as hair or brief as breath,
I want to squeeze the book shut,
tuck it under my arm, bring it
with me where I go, read it
on the meadow or in the rain
or in the crowded train, I want
to savor every word of it
in my own way until I understand
it and it understands me.

4 April 2022

Peel the Beginning Away

layer by layer,
lichen, time's
lipstick left on stone,
broken bandwidth, get
beyond the elements, all
the wise vascular improvisation
we call a living body,
find the before,
before the before,
the little snicker
of the oldest furthest,
galactic synagogue where
some togethering was intended
and we did, we do, we came
along and chanted, what else
is human breathing but a canticle,
our never-ending psalm
praising the before the beginning.
That it began.

2.

Breath says I am praying
though I seldom know it,
praying undistracted by words,
concepts, images, ideas—
just praying, praying.

Religions try to help you breathe,
remind you bead by bead,
word by word, sacred syllables
to take your next breath
and let that breath bring you
closer to before the beginning.
And we know the sad
thing that happens when
someone stops praying.

3.I saw it once

in a hospital,
the last prayer
breathed out
quiet, the blood
stopped flowing,
nothing happened,
quiet, quiet,
my dearest friend was done.

4.

I grew up with a poem
that kept quoting
In my end is my beginning.
Critics spoke of circles,
sense of destiny, goal of living,
afterlife as when we really

start living, heaven and all that.
Maybe maybe maybe
do you like my mantra?
all of them and none of me
and what does my own breath
tell me? Between breaths
before spreads out,
vast green meadow
to the horizon where the next
breath waits, but on
this prairie I catch a glimpse
of someone waiting,
not coming towards me,
not moving much, turning
like a child looking around.
But not a child.

6 April 2022

What more can I tell you,
stone lasts a long time
but time lasts longer.
I know London and Paris,
Vienna and Berlin—not Rome,
not Athens. Doesn't that
tell you something?
The road is wet
the rain's all gone,
that old song.
There must be something
I can give you, random letters
cast out of silver or tin, tin
is easier to stick on the wall,
magnets on the fridge, what
are the letters spelling now?
Why do we do this to ourselves,
the clock, the calendar,
the names we glue on newborns,
all our ever-afters? And why
do I think I have to say anything
at all about this, or have
anything to say? The words insist.
O brothers and sisters, the words insist.

9 April 2022

The golden chariot goes by
with no one in it,
goes by overhead,
its horse is the wind,
a fierce shadow pounding by
silently overhead.
Its passage is news enough,
it wakes what sleeps inside us
and suddenly we are filled
with that alertness we call knowing,
just knowing. Be careful—
what we know might send us back to sleep.

10 April 2022

Watch the old window
walk around the woods
the world the weeds
and everything between—
everybody has one good window,
everybody has a tree
it takes maybe, maybe
more than one life to climb.
Guess what it means, don't make
me do all the work
although I dearly want to,
your bark under my hands.

2.

But the window is watching,
it pays to behave—
sit by the fire, sing to your mother,
and when that sun is shining
remember rain
just so that your other hand
feels something like love.

3.

That little word that means *complete*.
Finish the drawing, fill the glass,

drag my river all the way to your sea.
Without you I am only me.

4.

Forgive the intrusion of theory,
theory likes to slither into poetry
to make the reader think
instead of reading, relaxing
into the real what is read.
Thinking has been bothering us
two thousand years since
angry Greeks invented it,
ran out of Troys to destroy
and turned their spears
on the sounds that come
out of our mouths, myriad
pronunciations of a single kiss—
language. Forget the yelping
of those cynics, tear up their treatises,
just listen to lust and love and trust
one word at a time.
The word will do you.

5.

If I'm not mistaken
that's what the window says.
I am what happens,

I am what you see.
What I mean is what you do with me.
But I might be wrong, I too
sometimes forget to listen
and when you don't listen
you hear the strangest things.
So listen hard and listen soft
and sometimes let
the word listen for you.

6.

End of sermon, Sorry,
the sun made me do it,
it seems so clear, so spring,
so flowering. A tiny sprig
of lilac scented the whole room
last night when a friend brought it,
the first of the season, blossoming
on the first really warm day,
when you came back hot from a walk
and even I dared sit out in the sun
and all night the scent of lilac
did our thinking for us.

13 April 2022

Good Friday

The pain of it lingers still.
So hard to understand
how people could do such things,
that someone would let it be done.
We used to sit in church
from noon till three,
Tre Ore they called it,
three hours of Christ's suffering,
until his quiet came.
Centurion's spear then we
stumble out into springtime,
thirsty, wiping our eyes,
forsythia offering its gold.
Or so often huge grey skies
turbulent with cloud
and no wind, a sky like ruin,
end of the world, we walked
from one fear to another.
But a bus would go by
and then it was just another day.

2.

Today on the other hand
nothing happens.
Sky pale blue, calm sun
on the lawns. Slow change

of register in the neighborhood.
Barns with no cows,
silos with no grain.
What is this tune
the relaxed meadow
sings to its horizon?
Why is it so quiet?

3.

Inferences
abound.
They come from the mind
like flowers from the ground.
Wait till I see me
walking in the field—
then I will believe.
Wait till the blackbird
perches on the phone pole—
then I will listen.
The empty road whispers
how close I am to going away.

15 April 2022

The Artisan Called Before the Tribunal Deposed:

The touch is all I wanted,
one touch tells everything.
The surface *is* the core,
the heart throbs where you can see it,
only there. To touch
is to know, lay a finger on the skin
and the soul of the person
sings a canticle instantly
only the one who touches can hear.

As one glimpse of the sea
tells all we will ever really know
of what she is, our mother,
so one glimpse of a tree,
a mountain. We see
the entire universe
when we glance up at the sky.

Do you understand at last?
Your law books take much too long,
by the time you've read a few pages
you've forgotten the taste,
of the real, the touch.

19 April 2022

Tower

Corseted with flowers
the tower stands.
A modest tower,
even I can climb it,
clambering up the stone
steps inside to teach
a place above the flowers.
Me and sky together at last,
this beautiful assignation
coaxed by morning glories.
Not high above the earth
but high enough, air, sun
and all the other music of space
cleansing me, scrubbing
the me off me and letting
a man stand there in the simple light.

22 April 2022

He Said to Her

Be my river.

She answered:
I am the sea.

He:
There must be some way
that you can come to me
for I am where I am
and know no other way to be

She:
I'll tell you what to do—
close your eyes
think of sad things
—burned-down libraries,
lost religions, the woman
you forgot to approach—
until you weep, just a little
no need for anguish, just
a tear or two. Now open
your eyes and follow the tear
as it rolls down your cheek,
falls onto your wrist, rolls
off onto the ground beneath you,
starts to grow, grow wide,
and flow, it flows, grows,

flows, until you have a river
of your own. And one day
you will be able to move.
Then you can follow it,
follow it all the way to me.

22 April 2022

Give the angel
time to speak,
his clock is not like ours,
yours, even the bishop
keeps our same hour
and the rabbi and the lama
even, but the angel's
moment triangulates from ours.
Yours. Wait. The word
is coming, shaped
like a shaft of light, shadow
of a bird blessed upon us.

23 April 2022

Why do we have pasts,
that trail of stale crumbs
the ants follow to annoy us now?
Growl. Why can't it
just be now, with no beaky
shadow jabbing us from behind?

2.

Growl, as I remarked.
I flee from was into is.
Does that mean I flee from me?
You decide. You have a me too.
There's an ant crawling on your shoe.

3.

No easy way to resolve
these problems more
physiological than grammatical.
But grammar is all we have.
Or does it have us?

4.

Start again. When the past
catches up with me

I run like a crocodile,
lie like an ad on TV.
Anything but then. Anything
but who you are and who
you think I was. I am nobody.
Nobody yet.

5.

That's why we have closets,
to shove last year in
and the year before and before that
until there is a musty but nice
friendly smell in there
among the leather and the fur
the shabby cotton of past love.
Dark in here. In there, I mean,
comfy in its own way, to lean
onto the memories. Danger.
Growl. Get out and slam the door.
That ant is on my ankle now.

3 April 2022

Trusting blondly
the brunette earth
I have come
to my grey time
in a world turning green.
And they were all here
all the while,
crayons in a child's hand.

25 April 2022

How to Write

Hear a word
and follow it
as you would
a bluebird
through the woods.

Something like that.
All the trees it touches,
all the leaves
it lands among,
all the insolent
silences it makes sing.

And if you don't
hear a word
to start with,
pretend you do.
No one will know
and the bird will still fly.

26 April 2022

Why Are You Going?

Haven't you been away enough,
long enough to be here a while?
Away is such a charmer, music,
images, svelte characters,
swoony marketplaces, stone.
Yes, I understand the appeal
of marble and limestone, yes,
the ruined temples, black sand
by a strange sea, or the same sea
speaking weird languages, yes,
but here has here in it,
here is right here, underfoot,
my hand in your hand, here
has no glamor, only the magic of being.

27 April 2022

Phone lines quiver in the wind—
who hears that cello playing?
Wind the bow and earth
the old Cremona, listen
hard as we can to understand
what the air is saying, remember
they used to call a song an air,
aria, the breath inside us
in love with all out there.

28 April 2022

The Memory House

so famous in the Renaissance
has another meaning now.
Everything, anything
I remember is where I live.
Everything that ever happened
is still happening. All the lost
things cluster round,
almost palpable, heartfelt,
stuffed in the mind.
It all is lost but all still here,
my feet that make
the floorboards creak,
the door opens by itself,
the dead ask permission to come in.

9 April 2002

Sometimes the song goes on
by itself, breath's sediment
slipping from the lips,
the human hum finds words
as if by accident.
But which comes first
it's hard to tell.
And no one needs to know,
we are not scientists,
we are people singing naked in the woods.

29 April 2022

May Day

There was no night, no bonfires,
no old devils witched away.
Just now. The sun
rolled us out.
No Europe, no liturgy.
America. Just now.
Labor Day around the world,
not here. Sunday.
The way the bones of the head
feel in the hand, sunshine
cold. What is to be done?
The birds on the lawn
repeat Lenin's question,
the farmer shouts to scare
a woodchuck away from his mulch.
There's one church open in town still,
Episcopal, named for a rabbi
got into bad trouble with Rome.
Then. Not now. Not now.
The woodchuck runs
but will come back. Marmota.
Saint Paul said Do not conform
your mind to the system,
transform, seek the new mind.
Just now. Sky as blue
as a word being spoken,
so fresh, never heard before,

just like yesterday. Just now.
Walk by the little river,
wade in the light. Your hands.

1 May 2022

Broken Promises

The irises by the Jacuzzi,
we love you
for the way you talk,
you teach us
not to trust weather,
even be skeptical of stones,
are you always California?
Ease open the dark knot-
work of morning clouds,
I think that's what you told me,
let the rain out,
the multitudinous
element in us,
But then I was a child,
stood beside the window box, pansies,
leaned back against
damp cinderblock garage.
Hurt no tree,
take care of me.
And the stone lips, hips, of Phryne
posed as Aphrodite,
yes, yes, see the gods
in our friends,
Olympus is the body of the other,
where all deities abide.

2.

I haven't said a word all day
so don't know who I am.
You know the rule,
You are what you speak.
The cinderblocks
were like rainclouds,
Genghis Khan
drove his warriors
over the pages of my book,
the roses were just beginning.
Watch my fingers as I talk.

3.

Wine poured over the piazzas,
something being
celebrated,
a horse or a homecoming,
tables spread,
old man shouting over the fiddlers

We spill the milk
of herself the Sun!
We all of us together
are Her one child!

What a neighborhood
to grow up in,

satin blouses,
the Mass in Latin.

4.

More to come.
Insert weather here.
The Weimar Republic
has a way of persisting
and we know what comes from that.
Try again. *J'accuse*. Leave
the fascist envelope
unopened.
Letter litter,
walk it to the dumpster,
come back and sniff
evening settle on the lawn.
Some laws are absolute.
Now help me rise.

17 May 2022

Bassoons Peremptory,

trees tuning up
waiting for the lifted arm
of our attention.

Raindrops passing slow,
neums of an older music,
people walking on the road,

or are we part of the chorus
only, this language business
so full and florid on our lips,
did somebody else say
what I think I'm singing?

Where trees outnumber people
logic, exhausted, sleeps
a galaxy apart. It's raining,
sort of, or as Jack Spicer
would say, Believe the rain.

Means listen to it
as to the trees
the white cars passing
boys on the playground
breath in your windpipe,
listen with your heart wide open,

sacred story stretched out
on the ground, the song we share.

19 May 2022

Dvorak in Central Park
surrounded by pigeons,
Tesla in Bryant Park
feeding his favorites,
bird on his hat, two
on his knee! Days later
his pale favorite came
fluttering into his room,
and passed into light
before him. And even I
sat on Eastern Parkway
offering a few peanuts
from the little cellophane
sack to half a dozen
grey birds round me.
In Nature's Realm
he called it, Everyone
we feed survives in us
after. Everyone
we feed survives in us
after. Years deep into now
the raindove on our lawn
teaches us to stay.

24 May 2022

Woods my own
unconfined. Leaves
lead me in,
I am a tenant
of their shade.

2.

Can't make music here,
so much is here already.
Adjust your ears—
timbres tell
more than tunes.

3.

No address. Night
still finds me out.
And at home
late sun
lets leaf shadow sing
through the pale curtains
so I blink my eyes to listen.

24 May 2022

Memorial

1.

Day the mind of what?
We are caught to consider
as between strata of rock
the Id of a nation
pressing inward outward at once.

2.

He looks up from his desk
and says: I have seen that
cloud before. In the sky it was
even as now. This is history
and I am here to understand.
3.
Welfare chiseler
the right wing calls him
for daring to be paid
just for being alive,
and has nothing but words
to sell and who wants those?

4.

That's what is meant by geology,
sound presses sound

down till the word is formed,
then word presses word
until at last you can stand
on the assembled rock
and stare out to sea.
Jonah is coming in his submarine,
soon the word will take on meaning
—leave it to the border guards.

5.

None but the lonely heart
the old song sang,
only the lonely heart
knows what it means
to be alone. What
it means to be at all.
Sounds soft and sad and tender
but it is made of absolute fear.
Why am I here at all?
What can I do to help?

6.

Immerse in rapture
is the usual critique.
Remember war and try
to make heroes of what it kills.
A day like any other

soaked in quotations.
Be brave. Braceros
headed north to mind the corn.

7.

Then I thought I heard
her coming up the hall
but she was still asleep.
Then I heard a seagull cry
but I looked out and saw a crow.
O resemblance is a hungry child,
I want the sky to be the sea.

8.

Woods Road north of Tivoli
is the darkest road I know,
so deep in forest, slender,
dark even with the western sun
trying to pry its way
through trees fuller, richer
than I have ever seen them.

It's what a road is
that matters,
not where it goes.

30 May 2022

Rabbit, Rabbit

we say first day of a month.
So June begins,
a girl god from the Adriatic sky.
How strange we call our time
by Roman gods and emperors,
just numbers when we run out of names,
September, October . . .
Calendars frown at us
from the wall, fluttering pages,
fly-specked, warning us
that Time is not our own.
We are slow dancers
in a sluggish sequence
that suddenly, every now and then,
turns out to be now.
First day of a month named
for a Roman goddess
in a year counted from the birth
of a Jewish boy the Romans killed.
Maybe I should go back to sleep
and play with the rabbit.
1 June 2022

Fermata

The song forgets its words
like a faithless preacher
hums on and on.
But they'll come back
summoned by music.
You can't keep birds out of the sky.

2.

Children in back seat
of parents' sedan
out for a Saturday spin.
Opera on the radio—
is that how it begins,
all those voices in all that song
and not a word they understand?
Make the words up
all by yourself—what else
can a poor kid do?

3.

But once you say it
it stays said.
Words are like sandstone
that way, stand
in the desert ever after
waiting to be heard again.

4.

The family stops at a diner
a little east of Babylon.
Peanut for the girl, black
raspberry for older brother.
No ice cream for the grown-ups,
we still wonder why.
Around the ice cream cones
the kids improvise language,
noises, have something to say,
irritate the busy silences
of our public space.
What else is language for?

5.

The world is homeopathic
isn't it, we cure music
by listening to it,
purify language by rabbiting
on and on (cf. *Finnegans Wake*),
cure silence by keeping still
and loving it. Just for one
moment, under the locust trees.

4 June 2022

Strata

Walk out
outcrop
the rock is enough
call it an anticline
the curves of time
pressed on each other
year after year
the rock across the river

I used to climb such things
but now I know better.
The Rock's job is to stand there
my job is to stand here
thinking as hard as
that rock holds together
what the word said
year after year stone to stone
the endless mineral of our thought
focused, made to stand
out there outside me, beyond me
where you are
the only one I really mean.

4 June 2022

This month seems to be going by
fast, slipstream of days
or slope of time to tumble down,
wake late, sleep early, smile.

2.

Speed used to be our pal,
the swiftest spermatozoon
(what a word!) gets the girl
and so on. But now I wonder.

3.

I woke up thinking about
flying home from London
some years ago, and how
for all its speed, six hours
all the way to New York, weary
flight attendants trying to smile,
all the jet roar, airport flurry
flying seems so old-fashioned
now, fussy and antiquey
stage coach in the sky.

4.

Ovum grabs Zoon and they make
another life together
and call it me. You. Anybody.
TWA turns into DNA. Speed spills.

5.

From such confusions
Sunday plucks a cloudless sky,
mild pleasant breeze,
one blue and all the greens.
Slow down, it says,
we're not going anywhere,
speed just seems—
and I woke up thinking also
sub umbra alarum tuam
protege nos, protect us
under the shadow of wings,
dear God with wings,
such simple Latin,
not the wings of a passenger jet,
not even the wings of a bird.
The real wings. The here and now.

5 June 2022

Envisioning the Obvious

all over again,
imagining the actual!

Ah, there's the work of morning
read the scripture portion,
let the cows out of the barn,
one by one, no stampede,
now plant a tree.

2.

The couple in Catskill did that,
a dozen or so, each
a different kind, tree dialects,
tree colors, till the whole backyard
became a coat of arms.
Every morning it gleams
its motto out at the neighbors,
This is what we mean,
this is who we are.

3.

To the neighbors
and to the birds
who come to pick and choose,
a tree's a kindly bird trap

that lets them come and go.
But while they're there
they teach us music,
high tones to slip through dull ears.

4.

I get confused
sitting out among trees,
all those trees up there
and these right here,
all the languages they speak,
or is there only one
and I am numb?
Anyhow, I hear somebody talking.

5.

Morning. Eat food. Decide.
Imagine. Decide again.
There is choosing to be done,
a cloud comes over the trees.
Sometimes I feel so tentative,
caught between words and what
I think they mean, or I do, or
trees do, or where is music
when I need it most. Cloud,
dear cud, answer me.

6.

There was a life
when at this hour
speaking loosely
I would saunter
a few blocks north
to the subway and then.
And then all the rest of life begins.
Where are we going
when we stay at home?
Don't tell me there
is anywhere a state of rest.
It's all moving, what else can it do?

7.

Hence imagine carefully
what is already here,
pretend that 'here' means a place
not our feverish attention caught.

8.

I have written so many books—
does that make me a liar?
I was just writing down
what came to be heard inside.
So I put the words out there,
the way you'd lead cows

to pasture, or toss crumbs to birds.
I thrived on mere obedience,
a reasonably well-behaved child
with a few tantrums of silence.

9.

Come back and forgive me.
The reality of the rose
challenges the skeptic.
Along the shore of your island
right now at high noon
the *rugosa* are flourishing.
I am confident of this
though I'm 200 miles away,
I read my Bible, the dictionary
does not know how to lie.

10.

But that's not putting
the rose gently in your hand,
not gathering great bouquets
to make altars of your tables.
It makes me feel so guilty,
dear reader, forgive me,
I just say the words,
you have to do the work.

8 June 2022

Tracing Shadows on Paper

All the way to the other side,
the owl in the middle of the alphabet—
it would be like dreaming
of Robert Duncan giving a reading
from his poems written on the other side.
Yes, but it's only morning,
ordinary to look at,
I take dictation
from the nearby trees.

2.

Of course Athena's
was the bird of night,
how else could wisdom come
except when all the holy
distractions of the sacred senses
idled while we sleep,
quiet sedan purring in neutral
parked alongside the road
under the walnut trees.

3.

Talk to me about your dreams,
tell me everything
and don't forget the waking stuff,
bank account and manicure,

everything counts.
You know me, know what I crave,
absolutes and applesauce
and shapely shadows
moving on the window shade.

4.

Tell me the names
of people I used to know
until my fingers twitch
with reminiscence
and the elevator doors
sweep open and set me free
at a higher level,
the chromosomes of custom
cobbling a new personality
fit for the thirteenth floor.

5.

I was building in the night
and you were too,
someday we'll figure out
how to work on the same structure
so it will be there when we wake
and then the house
will gobble us up,
you thought it was an owl
I knew it was a mourning dove.

6.

Another name is rain-dove,
I like that better, I love rain,
I'm Irish, or English, or some
islandish thing that makes wet
the answer to most questions,
and no more grieving.
So the name matters
more than people realize,
nomen numen the Romans said
either noticing or making it up,
the name is a god.

7.

How far have we gotten in the alphabet,
we're at the house but can't
see through the window yet,
I know she's in there,
afloat in the Jacuzzi,
I know he's on a stepladder
tacking a quotation in big letters
on the dining room wall.
But I can't see her,
I can't read what it says.
I'll try the Greek alphabet instead.

8.

They've told me so much this morning,
I sing my thanks in husky baritone,
breadcrumbs on the window ledge,
my breath goes out to feed a cloud.
I'm on the other side already,
I hear the crows at last.
Winter was with us long,
even last week I wore my overcoat
so again I ask the window
When does now begin?
Sometimes I miss going to church,
funny smells and awkward people
all trying to be good
but long ago church came to me,
I have to be the congregation
and the priest and altar boys
and sexton all by myself,
a lot of work for a lazy man.
Trees have shadows.
Men have ideas.

9.

Maybe in the dream
he just recited alphabets
in that high, tender, West Coast voice of his,
letters in order, letters all mixed,

X's and Y's and Q's all over,
more than natural. But then he said:
I am nature—
be me if you can.

10.

Every now and then blank verse is best,
the gleaming fur of listening people,
you see the shimmer in the audience,
soft sucking of ears taking it all in
you think you hear them hearing you right back,
listeners, magistrates of your craft.
They're here to certify your loving lies.
The audience, closest you come to god.

11.

So give more readers,
use more letters,
O and N feel neglected
but you've done your best for Z.
Now learn Russian.
Now play chess
the way you did once,
that virgin sport
that has no children,
just the ivory in your fingertips,
never stop touching me.

12.

When a bird passes overhead
and you know it only because
you see its shadow down below
you'll seldom know precisely
what kind it was—so much
for ornithology of everyday life
as Freud would say.
Now learn to read shadows—
what was that science called again,
something like scenosophy?
And there's nowhere to look it up.
So you have to do it all yourself,
start on the other side
of wherever you think you are,
leave the comfy motel of now
and follow the shadow home.

10 June 2022

Ocean of Air
for Apollinaire

the waves of it
find us, touch us
everywhere
no way to hide
from their caress
they teach us
we are here to be touched,
we would not live
without their embrace.

10 June 2022

Say Yes to what is offered
even if it's weird
as long as it's not wrong.
Break no laws, hurt no one,
and everything else that comes
along is from the angels,
your own angels, not Rilke's,
you can touch them whenever
you feel your bare skin
suddenly, unexpectedly, arm
or rib or thigh, that is the angel
reminding you they're there,
 they're there, and there is here
and here is everywhere.

11 June 2022

The Tree Said to Me:

Why are you always
waiting for somebody else?
I stand where I am
and always.
And all I ever need
comes to me—air and water,
wind and rain,
birds of all languages,
little animals climb me,
and gorgeous pollinating
butterflies that rest so
like the flowers they elicit.
And we trees talk to one another
underground, root tip to root tip
and something more (I can't
tell you about it yet), swift,
easy as your phone and internet,
and all beneath the earth,
song and scripture, wake or doze.
No more do we need,
the word is enough,
no need to travel,
everything comes to us,
that's why we stand here.

13 June 2022

Postcards from My Ninth Year

Whiffletree
sky dark
wagon full of beets

❀

it could be Jordan
shallow sluice
cool to my ankles
stood on sun-bleached stones

❀

everything is next
nothing is now
can't help crying

❀

child means
water still tastes good

❀

nothing comes to mind
oh I get it
the trees are still asleep

❀

they dream
or drink
the morning sun

❀

never talked to them
they talked to me—
am I still like that?

❀

the moment came
the black cow
turned and looked at me

❀

taste of milkweed sap
forbidden
always risk of knowing

❀

scrupulous churches
why so many, people
only one priest

15 June 2022

At a certain hour of the morning
the sun drains the blue
out of the beech leaves
and the whole tree turns gold.
All the blue becomes the sky
beyond, adobe, time
playing with colors like a child.
But what a child!

5 June 2022

Memory

Lesser organisms
of beast desire—
scarecrow on the cornfield
long time no see—
bikini drying on a clothesline,
remember that rope
slung between city houses,
clothy telephone?

2.

But now is now
is wind playing
in the trees
or is it the trees
playing with it—
no man can tell.

3.

We can always try
to start again,
midsummer murmurs
rises soon,
everything is on the way.
But will I understand it
when it comes?
And will it know me?

4.

Memory, that ramshackle
museum with the drowsy curator,
Corinthian columns supporting
a thatched roof
somewhere in Donegal
where the girls are half-seal
and the gorse hedges
march around the fields at night.

5.

But love likes new things too.
There is a cellar under everything,
old brick walls, a barrel of wine,
a cloister of rats. Believe!
Each word emerges
and is right to do so,
no God but God
and we are at last where we are—
who dares quarrel with
the earth beneath their feet?
Our main business is inhaling all the time.

16 June 2022

Forget Everything.

A pheasant runs across the road.

The trees have changed
subtly in the night—
something they heard maybe
from the new moon.

Something is new,
breeze in the leaves,
wake with sweaty collarbone,
what then?
                              The visitor
will notice the murals
on all the walls keep changing,
the ceiling of the dome
keeps improvising colors—
don't bother trying to name them.
Rest your weary eyes now—
enough that you have seen the bird.

1 July 2022

It's not all automatic.
The mail has to find you,
the phone has to learn how to sing.
You are a moving target
even when you're sitting still
pretending to be peaceful
reading the paper
like your father fifty years ago.
Here is your license to let go.

2.

The Wizard of Yes
has brought you to this place,
this pace, this peace.
You always said his name.
You wonder sometimes even now
what the Witch of No would have,
could have, done for you, with you,
in you. The colors of passing cars
are all you have to go by now.

3.

Help everyone. Hurt nobody,
not even the hovering mosquito
hungry, wondering if it dares.
The rest will take care of itself.

1 July 2022

To a Dear Friend

Stay away or you'll
catch moonrise from me
when all the stars
slip off the sky
and only one green glow
is left to make
everything the same.

2.

Edges wander. Words
dissolve, ice
is just water, water
is just wet. You look
up at the empty sky
and ask, trying to be brave,
what happens next?

3.

What happens is more questions.
Even when no answer ever comes,
there is some comfort in asking.
Asking makes energy. Answers mute.

4.

Then one day I heal again,
the stars come back,
definitions work again,
a wheel is round.

4 July 2022

Limits

1.

Fence round the organ
let no sound out,
let it stay inside
heaven of pure hearing
with nothing heard.

2.

Luminous void
from which we come
to the gathering
(*ecclesia chiesa église*).
Some call it the lord's
house *(kuriakou,
kirk,* church) but he
is everywhere
and we are for this
lifelong moment
only here.

3.

So listen softly
to the edge of things,
the edge is where the taste

is truest, where
things meet,
soft explosion of being here.

6 July 2022

Try the opposite,
the wet road,
the skimming blue jay,
hay her it sounds in Germany,
who is she? She is who's blue.

2.

Glisten. Glacier
did this rock,
leaf on leaf the stone,
readying the place
for us it would seem.
Detecting purpose
is a devious art,
a tale we tell we never heard.

3.

We walked there
shuffling through the numbers
a little unsteady underfoot.
East, west numbers look the same
and that's just part of our problem.
Where does this road leave
I used to say as a child
mishearing the word lead,

it leads to here it leaves me
but where is that? Only
the trees seemed to know,
tall black pines outside Callicoon.
Enough of me. Lead, leave,
I just stood still.

4.

For I am glacier too,
change where I am
and where I pass.
And you are too,
there is more stone in us
than most suppose.
We are chemicals plus something more.

7 July 2022

Fragments of Stained Glass

Angels like ospreys
carry to heaven

we are digested by pure light

❋

He is as big as the sky
the whole sky
not just what we see of it

in front of him
a woman ran to us
red, riding on a trinity

❋

on a wet brick wall
vine with blue grapes
each grape a window

❋

No knife needed
to cut this bread
no cup needed
to drink this milk

if it is milk—no one knows,
it is white and it flows.

❋

Theology begins
by understanding
the parts of the beloved's
body, touch their thigh
and you'll know why

❋

colors always
tell the truth—
did you know that?
I think you are blue.

❋

what is a church?
a house on a hill,
damp basement,
wind in the attic
and by the broken window
a mourning dove
coos those words
five at a time
over and over

if you want to be
in you must come out.

✸

The self is battered
from all sides,
give up the self
and just be
and the whole world will be at peace.

14 July 2022

Opal

1.

And we are magistrates of fact
or light, call it by its old Venetian name
a white church on a blue lagoon.
Names rule us, and we rule the names.
Byzantine satisfactions of being wrong
then letting the light correct us,
skin and all, bronze and melody,
look in our hands and remember.

2.

Lucky that tigers have stripes,
and did the sea reject the island
or did the rock shrink away from the sea?
The child thinks: No reason for reality,
it's all a grown-up's trick
to keep me in my place—
adults, is that what adultery really means?

3.

The signal when it comes
will be a gull on the roof beam.
The sea is made of faces,
you even know some of their names.

4.

Good at grasping,
flight holding on,
raptors, hunt from the sky,
swoop down out of the light—
the eagle, the osprey, and what about me?
we grab more than they even do.
Rapacious she called us
then she went away.

5.

If Irisher I'd fiddle
to say all the rest
but I'm pale and
have to word it out.
Think of a word
as an opal—brilliant,
precious, never
entirely translucent,
clear and cloud
chorus of one.

15 July 2022

Augury

The fauna of belief
run through the rocky valleys
where you choose to sleep.

No clouds, except puffs of dust
when a big one lands,
flurry of wings
you scurry to interpret.

Rhyme rules. Hurry home.
Once you hear the cry
you need to know why.
And so on. Sit on a seaside
boulder, solemn throne.

Remember what panic really means:
everything we touch
turns somehow into us.

Real things are contagious—
only in nightmares are we safe.
All of us are begging bowls—
feed me, feed me.

25 July 2022

Ipseity

If I needed a religion
would you be there for me?

Derangements of piety,
feed the birds, let the wife weep.

Early we learn to
go hungry and at least be me,

that fabulous person
they shout and whisper at so much

until he almost believes he is a self
but not quite the self they mean.

I'm still learning who I mean
when I say me.

2.

Don't be so fussy
about identity,
things come and go.

Music in the air
from somebody else's radio,
a dog barks, a shade
rattles in the wind—

How can you work all that
into your story,
the one you tell yourself
and shyly hope and pray
some other people read it too?
Don't you sometimes
feel like just sitting there?

26 July 2022

Tao Tale

Lao-tzu on his ox
we ride the animal we are
into the wilderness
where words lead

or we can fall
into the silence
between one word and the next

paradise of quiet
at the end of every line of poetry.

The ox moves slow
beneath the burden
of human wisdom
thighs of an old man
squeezing its flanks.

His name is playful,
sounds like *old child,*
newborn wisdom
on creaky knees
that need the ox
to get there, where
the sense in silence lives.

2.

But Jesus walks with us
on his broken feet,
iron spike through ankle bone,
no ox, no mule to shuffle
into Jerusalem. He moves east,
his own feet half an inch
above the road, he walks
the way Romans saw their
gods going, *incedere,*
walk without touching the ground.

3.

I wonder if they met along the way,
never mind history, time
is wax in our hands, melt it,
shape it, chill it firm again,
only space matters,
maybe they met in Bactria or Tibet.
The books don't tell.
Only the silence speaks.

26 July 2022

Beach pebbles
come in all sizes,
instruct us
in the processes
by which they came to be.

Why are they so smooth?
Why do we take them home,
enshrine them, half worship them?
The density of time
turned into opaque gems,
all the more precious
because they are outside
money, system, policy, dogma—
they just are.

So if this were a sermon
it would try to explain
how on this one pebble
my wife stubbed her toe,
while on that bigger one
Aphrodite sat first time she ever
came ashore from the surf
where she was born,
but with that hefty rock
there Cain smote upstart Abel.
And on that big white stone

Christ stood before rising into heaven.
And no one can prove me wrong!
Anything is possible, we live
among the likely, you never know.
Only the stones really know.

27 July 2022

Kindling

Kindle. Call
for the memory.
Quick walker up the hill
but what have you
done for me lately?
Shop-Vac suck up ashes
maybe, sprinkle of
what is that wet
that comes before rain?
Walk faster. She needs
your answer, images will do,
just say who, faster,
your shadow is at your heels.

2.

Late twelve-tone music
strict numbers, lax sounds,
tuneless, adrift. O better
the daisy, bend low to retrieve
the simplest flower,
tell your telephone
isn't there a tune in it
somehow could whistle?
All voices of a fugue in one hum?

3.

Auden on Cornelia,
Olson on Fort Square
Duncan on Nineteenth.
The triangle affair,
the luscious lisping lips
of all unlikeness
speaks a whole city out
bigger than the nation
it lives in, because
and just because
a city stretches as far
as you can hear or understand,
no frontier, no stupid
border guards like me
smoking smuggled cigarettes.

4.

Well, we had come back from Asia
Delhi to Dubai to the Black Sea
and then up the river to Vienna.
One more novel written in sleep.
But still, picture me at dawn
looking out at the Persian Gulf,
ninety degrees already
among all the white buildings.
What did I see?

I should have asked
that Iranian water
what makes me me,
because it has seen so much,
sad birds, drifting
rafts of unchronicled despair.

5.

It has to go on,
you can't stop now
so close to the top
of what you think is a hill.
Boundaries in the sky!
Lazy lovers in their sweaty beds!
Skateboard snarling down asphalt!
Liberty Bell cracked from the start—
how fragile to be free.

6.

Could this then be a cenotaph,
an empty tomb of one
whose bones are somewhere else?
Is that why school is so boring,
Scraps of words
stitched together
stamped in fragile
sheets of paper

stitched together
and call it truth,
biblion, book?
I put it in your hand,
trust me, it is my hand.

7.

In Vienna that basement room
where princes of the blood
are entombed, neatly,
close together, inscribed,
and upstairs a busy street goes by,
ordinary as applesauce,
you know, the way it slips
cool sweet twixt teeth and cheek.

8.

When I was a kid
one of the things I loved to do
shoot arrows at cardboard boxes
yards away in a vacant lot.
Now I call it writing words,
careful, careful, people
moving in the middle distance.
I loved the hollow thump
the box made when the arrow hit.

9.

I think the walker won his hill,
no sign of him now, or her,
whoever that was, o now
he's coming down again,
slow, slow, as if regretful
to be leaving whatever it was
the sky disclosed,
or what else is up there
you'd run so fast to see?

10.

In London they say mews,
the houses behind the horses,
they whisper the truth
by spelling it awry, the tunes
the grace, the meanings
all come from behind us,
or we are the shadows truth casts
shadows that mingle
with one another, each hoping
to get the story right,
the one the Muse declared
and left us to articulate.

11.

Wait, I'm getting ultimate again.
It is Sunday after all
in a couple of hours a bell
will call a handful of maybes
to some sort of service,
I don't know what, I know
the beautiful mosaics on the wall,
the chapel's over there,
back beyond three houses, yes,
it all comes from behind our back,
the house behind the house
where all of us get born.

12.

Small craft advisory
all day today
they say.
                    I love
what people say
not always how they mean it but
the words! the words!
each one an encapsulated symphony
if I may be fancy yet again,
a song is in them
to say it simple,
a song is in them,
all you have to do is listen.

13.

Remember *La Bohème,*
first act, Paris garret, winter,
a writer burning his manuscripts
in the little stove to keep warm.
Music. The love story comes later,
Girl needs light, song and sorrow,
stick with the first act,
the opera's all there, man burning
words that he had put together,
words that once were his own.
Stick with the kindling,
listen to the crinkling as it catches
page by page, do it slowly,
one page at a time,
keep the music, keep the warmth
slower, one page burns as hot as ten,
stick with the kindling.
You never know who'll
come, lured by that warm
if feeble glow. The door
is ready to be knocked on.
Shiver, rub your hands, wait.

14.

Persia seems a long time ago,
I had a beard then, and rings
on my fingers, oil in my hair

and thought I was a priest
of a goddess who had not yet
told me her name before I woke,
in Vienna. In Munich. In Paris.
Or had she whispered it
and I forgot? Priesthood done with
I strolled along the Seine
glancing at stalls on the embankment,
books and more books,
old photos, engravings, more books, more books.
Watch the river instead,
try to look picturesque and Parisian
for gawkers in the tour boat passing.
Stay with the water,
let it do the running for you—
I think my grandmother
might have said that
but I never knew her
in real life, the phrase we use
to mean time, earth time,
more slippery than Seine.

15.

Man in white shirt
passing slowly by white wall.
Morning is magnificent.

16.

If I got into a boat
(scary enough)
and motored up the bay
to Woods Hole
I could meet a maven
who would explain
whether or not
the sea has boundaries
of its own built in—
if I were a fish could I swim
anywhere on earth I wanted to?
Or are there zones I know not,
not just sharks and leopard seals
but some immense awareness
of where to be and where not.
Can the ocean tell me that?
I asked that of the Persian Gulf
but it was too busy with history
to notice my mere speculations.

17.

So it always comes back
to this hill, this place
where earth swells up
a little closer to her sky.
Beautiful breeze today,

grackles on the deck
quiet for a change.
Cloudy light, green
shimmer in the bushes.
Enough. You know
where I am, now
no need to guess who.
Location is identity.

7 August 2022

When the organ plays
in the empty church
it makes the pigments
in the murals wake.
I try to sneak in those times
to watch the music
but something always senses me,
maybe the stone walls
or those bright windows
full of watchful saints,
so by the time I slip into a pew
the paintings on the wall
calm down again, as if to say,
we are just images, don't
put too much faith in us
though we are made of colors
and color is made of truth.

8 August 2022

As if the rhythm
understood all by itself
what the cloud meant
to the finches
chattering below,
busy as a gamelan
and who, really who
is that who is listening?

2.

The rhythm knows.
Out there are rocks,
in here are dreams—
I stubbed my toe on one
and woke annoyed
at how it made me think
of what I wanted not to,
clumsy as a stumble
by the bedroom door.

3.

Then I really woke and wrote
a book called *The Triangle:*
Find the Point Where Dreams Live.

Stupid title unless I make it true.
Outside, the working men
are making all the noise they can,
the finches fled.

Can't I talk about the morning too?
Is it only the government
that owns the hours of the day?
Go back to rhythm,
little heart, count the beats
and swim along between,
hasten to the silences,
little brain, make yourself
at home in all of them.

9 August 2022

Cloud Language

We left the cloud
to take care of the sky
and ran inside.
We are revolutionaries
trying to turn everything
upside down, but quietly,
and only because
we like the underside of things,
the road behind us, the unseen.

2.

Yes, you're right,
I am speaking of religion.
But it is not me speaking,
is it? It's really you
understanding, *n'est-ce pas?*
That sounds too easy.
It's neither you nor me.
It's the thing itself talking,
cloud language, bone language,
the old saint said Faith
is to believe in what we have not
seen. I'd call it love instead—
the future is always behind us,
waiting, walking along with us.
But our necks don't swivel far—

only the owl can spin its glance
all the way back—
that's why they call it the bird
of Athena, goddess of wisdom.

3.

We're walking behind someone
or following them up the stairs
we suddenly know them,
something about them, vividly
felt, utterly convincing,
but impossible to put in words.
We know at that moment
a thing they don't know themselves,
we've seen their fact or future
scribbled down their backs.
Lucky for them and for us
we've run out of words.

13 August 2022

North Bay

It's near the river
but it isn't the river,

it's all the same water
but it doesn't go.
It lingers with us, idle
kayak, a raft will just
shimmer a little
and not depart,
a piece of paper will
float, words up,
still readable.

2.

Along the shore mallows grow,
color a vibrant mauve
(their name in French,
Latin *malva*, color of a blush).

3.

So many things I want
to tell you about this bay,
riverine lagoon, placid pool,
the train tracks beyond

seem to keep it safe
from the tidal river
washing it away. A bay.
A bight. A tender cloud
in the sky of earth.

4.

I want to be there now,
snug on shore, cool morning,
water clean enough to swim
the mavens say, but I don't,
water is a church I pray outside.

5.

We walked there more than once
but all the visits blend into one,
we're looking for something,
bird? tree? flower? mushroom?
who knows what, we walked
through the two meadows
then down the wooded headland
to stand there, just looking,
and a train went by. We always
seem to see them heading south,
eis ten polin, to the city,
not Is-tan-bul now, New York.

6.

But you can never tell.
Sometimes the City
is right here, is every
place that summons our senses
and teaches us to know
this landscape or this lover
and what that knowing means.
This little marshy pond
by the Hudson our metropolis.

14 August 2022

Ornithosophy

A wren at evening
who am I fooling
wake to cars slishing
up wet morning road
but it isn't raining
we live together
radiant from Earth
slivers we all are
of the Sun's hard light
enough to stand the dark
and come again
I think it was a wren
or someone looked like her
and why not, the day
is very large, evening sigh
chittering finches at dawn
wave the window
at the trees

2.

and these others
who grow behind my back
heart-shaped habit
of profusion, shadow cool,
caught between things
the teeth of words

3.

so we hear the poultry
in nobody's yard
grace grace the accent
changes with the time of life
the empty rowboat
drifts back to shore
stare at the park bench
till it tells you all
lovers losers kindly folk
absent-minded feeding
pigeons at their toes
these weathered wooden
slats your history book

4.

or any bird at all
history is just ornithology
of our flightless species
how we got there anyhow
over Bosporus or broad
sacred Atlantic to be
anywhere at all
man is a migrant
she gets up and goes

5.

flightless words?
let the queen decide
she has been here
longer than stone
yesterday's tempest
in the river of our trees
but the road is dry today
quiet as can be
apart from the liturgy of leaves

6.

remember that
when we shake hands
we bring to each other's skin
all the places we have been
no wonder we bump elbows
now in plague time
but bones have been somewhere
too, the body knows
all too well the world it's in
maybe all that hair and skin
is just a message from the bone
but meaning what?
always looking for meaning
like a kid for a candy
meanings don't nourish us

only the searching does
migrations forever
raindove on the railing
we're there already
but never know it

7.

Amplitude of evidence
bulge in the pocket
cloud in the north
it costs so much to remember
even without a therapist
lines of the face
tribunal of her angry eyes
he wanted to speak
without using words
wound up using
words without speaking
stories like that
whispered in bathroom stalls
scratch your name
on metal door and wonder why

8.

Remember mucilage?
used to stick things together
weaker than glue

but it worked, but it's
up to things to agree
to be cobbled together
marrying papers together
the hidden dark
crinkling in between them
o marriage marriage
high priest of the temple
your wife is your pontiff
and you'd better know it

9.

what did they tell you
about me when they sent
you out to lead me home?
did they warn you
to bring some silence with you?
you were a wren at the window
that didn't do it so
a woodpecker next time
so now we're even
we have awakened each other
and it's still only Friday
late for breakfast again
can't remember what I ate
only the news of the day
they dared to call it
slopped down beside my plate

10.

but I grew up with sidewalks
fire hydrants the only
wildlife the dog down the block
but the sea was near enough
to walk down and see
and that is my whole story
the mafia of the public library
enlisted me half
against my will but my want
was so strong it chained me
to the next book and the next
and then I went to France
and who knows what happened
then but enough about me
I was only here to reassure you
someone can speak a word
or two and still survive,
the ninety-nine inning ballgame
nowhere near its end

11.

or was it poltergeists
I meant I heard
rustling the cellophane
drives you up the wall
in my nightmare

I hear a blasted basketball
bouncing slow and regular
on asphalt, young men
are demons, I was one
but hated a ball I couldn't
hold, squeeze in one hand
the subway roared
beneath the corner
you could hear it sometimes
when wise folk came to visit
and lecture from my leather chair
who needs to know any more?
sufficient to the day
is the evil thereof
I asked the priest
and he explained
what Jesus meant
and all I carried away
was a word of the day
is enough to say
or one word says it all

12.

but enough about birds
my wife knows them so well
can whistle in a dozen languages
from Towhee to Oriole
she can sing them down to feed

takes gorgeous pictures of them
I study the images
until the color sinks in
from what I see
but enough about me
you read poetry to learn
a wider world than
the one that only
seems to be here
sink into the word
the empty boat will float you
all the way to the shores of
the land of Goshen
what is that? a racetrack
in the country, a childhood
forever coming back?
settle down softly
in the empty boat
a word is waiting for you.

19 August 2022

Waiting for the discus
to scuttle down out of the sky
two thousand years pass.
Gibraltar endures
half a dozen languages,
the sea is a strict grammarian,
don't you forget it, Julie,
next time you 'borrow'
somebody's canoe. Kayak
weather yet to come. Waiting
for the lute strings to snap
at last and the interminable
improvisations meet their term.
But music never ends,
just goes inside, rat
in the floorboards of the mind.
You can almost see the discus
or whatever it is on its way,
a shimmer whirling
low over the meadow. The grass
has been waiting too, sheep
after goat after aurochs,
we're getting there,
on the Pacific Palisades,
speaking German, remember?
His vocabulary did this to him
Spicer said, in the wheelchair,

in the elevator, a boy from Idaho
always ready to pick up the song.
I remember getting off the train
in Pocatello, finding my old
friend now a young mother,
Mormons everywhere, the ghost
of Ed Dorn still living in the air.
The lute string snapped then,
chronology falls apart when
you look too close, don't kiss
the calendar, you never can tell
where or when it's been.
Throwing means thinking,
catching the ball means knowing.
The discus is on its way
but no one dares to catch it,
keen-edged, whirling knife,
let it finally come to earth
and show you where, if
by luck or chance you're there.
Sometimes you wake at night
and hear ancient Sparta
slipping fast through the sky.

20 August 2022

Just for a moment
suppose the sea
Or not just now,
let it last, vast,
covering most
of the globe, sea
always leaving
some room for us.
For you and me.
Now suppose me,
insignificant indeed
but at your side.
Where things are
sometimes means
more than what they are.
Suppose the sea again
now and be at peace.

21 August 2022

Words get simple to confuse me.
I'm trying to rebuild a whole culture
starting with stones I find
all over the ground, pluck
without much effort, chips
that happen to resemble
ruins of Athens, pavements
of Jerusalem, whatever I need,
shadows of Glastonbury,
your pearl earring on the carpet,
come out of Eden, begin again.
I'm drowning in simplicity.

2.

But what else could words be for
but to create a lasting nation
urgent with kindness
and luminous permissions?
Land of no lying, country of no kill.
It's worth a try. Now start
forever again.

24 August 2022

The Small Things Again

And nothing easy.
The geology of everyday,
who made my mountain?
This syncline in the mind,
all those experiences
pressing down together,
graceful thunder weight of rock
bending the moment, the old
Who-am-I-today spring
trickling down the shale.
Too much to remember with
such weak fingers, too far
ahead to think with such bones.

2.

The dream made simple sense:
a tall slim outfielder not only
hits the long ball but steals
bases too. Strength I guess
and speed and knowing where
to be and when to go.
Roma, rope a jenny to your caravan,
it's actually always time to go.

3.

A mule, a mile, a breakfast on the move,
spit out the cherry pits, the field
is interested in new trees,
roadside manners,
life is the silent wolf
slouching greedily behind.

4.

But am I there yet
is a more plausible question.
Location outweighs identity.
Timing is trickier—is *now*
truly when you think it is?
Each being has its own now.

5.

We failed geology
but want the earth
to be soft as shoes
and easy as a spoon.
A cup. A bowl. A lake
in the oasis, shade
of a handy tree.
Presumptuous to the last,
when I say we I mean me.
What do *you* mean?

6.

I asked the stone that once
in New Hampshire,
it glistened in the sparkles
reflected off the rushing stream
beside us both, and then
it hummed back at me
soft as a guitar, O little boy,
meaning is just a human thing.

29 August 2022

The rose opens the door
the wind decides to come in
just a little, just enough
for the star of petals
to set free the fragrance
that comes and grows at last
into a single knowing,
a flower of our own now
grows safe inside us.

29 August 2022

Hide the text inside itself
and then she said
Sit on the rock till you remember

✹

Wash the basin,
erase the stains
along the rim. Who
bled here? Whose
wine did we drink
and it was no accident?

✹

The wax the fingers
mesh together
on the chest of someone
asleep in sunshine—
no worse than that,
the words lock,
sometimes it's hard
to spread them apart.

✹

To the graduate student
I recommended she study

the way Welsh and English
poetic traditions influenced
each other even well before
the Nineteenth Century.
But she said: But I'm
working in organic chemistry!
so I said Precisely.

❋

Wrap thing in thing
until it's there,
smear gobs of ointment
on to find the skin.
The target summons the arrow.
But the fountain forever
misses the naiad they took away.

❋

No way we can have
one without the other.
A word means what happens
when you read it. Hear it.
Trust me, you are the dictionary.

❋

That's where we went wrong,
made the poor English teacher

sit on a stool in the corner
facing the wall. But angles
are always interesting, wrong
turned out to be just another
detour on the road to Jerusalem
and here we are.

30 August 2022

Not much to say today
so the words are free to come
streaming their sounds out
so we can share. Dare to.
Listen to them, not to me,
Opening a notebook
is opening the birdcage door
and all the sounds fly out—
and once a sound is on the wing
it never stops till you stop hearing
and even then something's left,
a rhyme, a name you remember
from childhood, sounds like
you know better than I do.

2.

Axe handle but the blade is gone.
Curious shapely wood, a little
like the leg of an antelope, say,
but with no jut of bone. A curve
in the world, smooth pale wood.
I can almost feel it in my fingers
but wonder what I'm thinking.
Wood has its way with us,
dreams its way into our hands.

3.

Axe handle came from X,
I was just looking at the letter X,
stands for Christ, for ten, for
multiply, like 2 times 5, stands
for Time's History on Russian
magazine, crossed arms, legs,
crossed fingers, the spot marked
to which all yearning hastens,
an old peasant's signature.
And then I heard a raven calling,
sunny morning, delivery truck
paused at the door, no X in sight.

4.

See what I mean when I say
I have nothing to say?
Means you have all this to hear,
matter of the mind, sounds
spilled on the sidewalk,
harbor full of ships from nowhere
laden with goods and grain.
And all of them for you,
for the city you are.

31 August 2022

Scream your head off
all you like
we used to say
and looked the other way.
Ignore complaint.
The forest of desire
subtends the mountain of fear,
hills of anxiety.
What does subtend mean again,
I remember her from school
if you didn't love her
you wouldn't worry—
simple as that? Not exactly,
think of the way Schumann
subtends Brahms, say,
or how at the end of his life
Duncan took Brahms as his master,
learn the piano, climb the cliff,
you have more than one life to give.

2.

Never mind the angles,
geometry is a wishful dream.
There are no straight lines
anywhere. The house
subtends your habits.
But the dream subtends the day.

3.

I watched them shovel coal.
I watched them up on scaffolds
washing tall buildings. I watched
them washing our car in tunnels
full of gush and spray excitement.
Watching is like being in church.
Prayer is watching with other eyes.

4.

So when I ignore complaints,
mostly my own but yours too
alas, I mean the dream, night
or day, makes things happen.
Go back and dream again,
I tell myself, and all this
will be better, Or different
at least. Nothing is the same.
The wind comes through the trees.

1 September 2022

Marconi on the Nova Scotia cliff
a signal sent, time slips past,
the message still on the way,
a galaxy is an idea in mind
not all that astro-stuff, I just
want to think about the sea
o'er which his message passes
like some old rhyming verse,
gospel hymn or Jordan jive,
come from where we live all
the way to where we are. Think
of an Historical Event. Scare
the daylights out of your cat.
Hear Bismarck's voice on an
incomprehensibly old recording,
yes, Hamilton shot Aaron Burr
and became Emperor of Mexico.
I mean Marconi is still there,
cold wind whipping up his knees,
still doing his magic tricks
so the Old Countries can hear.
And what does any message ever
say but I am here? Wake up,
it was cold last night, the heat
came on while we slept, History
had slipped out and was gone
forever, left the door open behind.

2 September 2022

If I were permitted
to lay the deepest
pleasures of my life
before you,

                                    mountain streams
and operas, afternoons in Avignon,
skin close to skin,
the taste of water,
the sound of rain,
the ardor in the heart
in the middle of the Mass,
the first time I read Coleridge,
I would gladly set them,
neatly as my clumsy heart allows,
before you as an offering
to you who somehow, how
I still can't figure out,
embody all of them
and promise even more
with the far light in your eyes.

5 September 2022

After I tell you
what it said
will you tell me
what I mean?
That's what love
is supposed to do,
teach me what
I'm on earth for
by studying you
until I can grasp
the work required
as birds explain the sky.

8 September 2022

What the sea spells
I have said before
listening with my child ear
rapt along the shore
or brought home to hum
in the little tin pail
the back of my head,
occipital symphonies!
grown-up words to say
what the oldest animal
my mother told me
so I could, let me, tell you.

27 September 2022

The private life of a pronoun
shows a little on the subway,
how it leans against the door,
swings from a strap, sways
with the shuddering train
or presses back against the pole
or sits demurely eyes in a book
or gazes frantically at all the rest
yearning for its verb to come.

29 September 2022

Flumina

When I was a kid
I was all about rivers,
wanted to know them,
cross them, sometimes even
float in a boat on one
a few minutes of its long day.
Shallow Delaware upstate,
vast Hudson sprawling
through our harbor into ocean,
the East all green and oily
and they said it was no river
but the sea, but good enough
for me. A river comes from
and goes to, and moves slow
enough for me to see
everything that was and will be.
And they had names! Rivers
I would never see, Orinoco,
Irrawaddy! Their names alone
carried me along, children
are rafts, everybody knows that,
and there we float and some
keep going. I live in the grace
of what I have been given,
a house with a window, from it
I can see the slim Metambesen
slipping down to be the Hudson.

29 September 2022

The calibrations of desire
required by a trembling leaf
remind us of language,
translating Proust, finding
the right words to talk to God
on the confessional or on
the podium where angels
listening surround us
disguised as us. The leaf
quivers in the least breath.
What do you ask of me
it asks of us, how can you see
me in all my immaculate
identity and not revise
the structure of your will,
your wants, needs, grasp
of your hands as you reach out,
your fingers trembling too?

26 September 2022
from & for Charlotte

Acknowledgments

A few of these have appeared in the journals *The Swan, 24 Hour Store,* and *Caesura.*

About the Poet

Robert Kelly was born in Brooklyn in 1935, father an accountant who sang, mother taught grammar school. Where else could he go but poetry? He went to a Jesuit school then CCNY and Columbia, classics, linguistics. Came to actual poetry through Coleridge, Pound, Yeats, Rilke, Duncan, New York in the 50s sustained him with joyous comrades, Blackburn, Antin, Rothenberg. After working as a translator (German, technical) for a few years, he was invited to teach for a year at Wagner College, then for the rest of his academic life, sixty-one years at Bard College, where he was blessed with incredibly creative students who allowed him to urge them towards poetry. If he could list their names, it might be a truer index of his work. In any case, he has written close to a hundred books of poetry, fiction, essays, even a play or two, and has started several little magazines (*Chelsea Review*, *Trobar*, *Matter*). In the past decade the main work was the five volumes of poetry he called *The Island Cycle* (*Fire Exit*, *Uncertainties*, *The Hexagon*, *Heart Thread*, *Calls*), and in this past year a long poem *The Cup*, and *Shadow Talk*, a score of fairy tales.

Kelly lives in the Hudson Valley with his wife, Charlotte Mandell, translator of Proust, Enard, Littell, Nancy, Blanchot and so many more, and editor of *Metambesen*, a pioneering venture publishing books and chapbooks of poetry online.

Black Square Editions was started in 1999 with the intention of publishing translations of little-known books by well-known poets and fiction writers, as well as the work of emerging and established authors. After twenty-four years, we are still proceeding book by book.

Black Square Editions—a subsidiary of Off the Park Press, Inc, a tax-exempt (501c3) nonprofit organization—would like to thank the following for their support.

Tim Barry
Robert Bunker
Catherine Kehoe
Taylor Moore
Goldman Sachs
Pittsburgh Foundation Grant
Miles McEnery Gallery (New York, New York)
I.M. of Emily Mason & Wolf Kahn
Galerie Lelong & Co. (Paris, France)
Bernard Jacobson Gallery (London, England)
Saturnalia Books
& Anonymous Donors

Black Square Editions

Richard Anders *The Footprints of One Who Has Not Stepped Forth* (trans. Andrew Joron)
Andrea Applebee *Aletheia*
Eve Aschheim and Chris Daubert *Episodes with Wayne Thiebaud: Interviews*
Eve Aschheim *Eve Aschheim: Recent Work*
Anselm Berrigan *Pregrets*
Garrett Caples *The Garrett Caples Reader*
Billie Chernicoff *Minor Secrets*
Marcel Cohen *Walls (Anamneses)* (trans. Brian Evenson and Joanna Howard)
Lynn Crawford *Fortification Resort*
Lynn Crawford *Simply Separate People, Two*
Thomas Devaney *You Are the Battery*
Ming Di (Editor) *New Poetry from China: 1917-2017* (trans. various)
Joseph Donahue *Infinite Criteria*
Joseph Donahue *Red Flash on a Black Field*
Rachel Blau DuPlessis *Late Work*
Marcella Durand *To husband is to tender*
Rosalyn Drexler *To Smithereens*
Brian Evenson *Dark Property*
Jared Daniel Fagen *The Animal of Existence*
Serge Fauchereau *Complete Fiction* (trans. John Ashbery and Ron Padgett)
Jean Frémon *Painting* (trans. Brian Evenson)
Jean Frémon *The Paradoxes of Robert Ryman* (trans. Brian Evenson)
Vicente Gerbasi *The Portable Gerbasi* (trans. Guillermo Parra)
Ludwig Hohl *Ascent* (trans. Donna Stonecipher)
Isabelle Baladine Howald *phantomb* (trans. Eléna Rivera)
Philippe Jaccottet *Ponge, Pastures, Prairies* (trans. John Taylor)
Ann Jäderlund *Which once had been meadow* (trans. Johannes Göransson)
Franck André Jamme *Extracts from the Life of a Beetle* (trans. Michael Tweed)
Franck André Jamme *Another Silent Attack* (trans. Michael Tweed)
Franck André Jamme *The Recitation of Forgetting* (trans. John Ashbery)

Andrew Joron *Fathom*
Andrew Joron *OO*
Robert Kelly *Linden Word*
Karl Larsson *FORM/FORCE* (trans. Jennifer Hayashida)
Hervé Le Tellier *Atlas Inutilis* (trans. Cole Swensen)
Eugene Lim *The Strangers*
Michael Leong *Cutting Time with a Knife*
Michael Leong *Words on Edge*
Gary Lutz *I Looked Alive*
Michèle Métail *Earth's Horizons: Panorama* (trans. Marcella Durand)
Michèle Métail *Identikits* (trans. Philip Terry)
Albert Mobilio *Me with Animal Towering*
Albert Mobilio *Touch Wood*
Albert Mobilio *Games & Stunts*
Albert Mobilio *Same Faces*
Pascalle Monnier *Bayart* (trans. Cole Swensen)
Christopher Nealon *The Joyous Age*
María Negroni *Berlin Interlude* (trans. Michelle Gil-Montero)
Doug Nufer *Never Again*
John Olson *Echo Regime*
John Olson *Free Stream Velocity*
Eva Kristina Olsson *The Angelgreen Sacrament* (trans. Johannes
    Göransson)
Juan Sánchez Peláez *Air on the Air: Selected Poems* (trans. Guillermo Parra)
Véronique Pittolo *Hero* (trans. Laura Mullen)
Pierre Reverdy *Prose Poems* (trans. Ron Padgett)
Pierre Reverdy *Haunted House* (trans. John Ashbery)
Pierre Reverdy *The Song of the Dead* (trans. Dan Bellm)
Pierre Reverdy *Georges Braque: A Methodical Adventure* (trans. Andrew
    Joron and Rose Vekony)
Valérie-Catherine Richez *THIS NOWHERE WHERE*
Barry Schwabsky *Book Left Open in the Rain*
Barry Schwabsky *Feelings of And*
Barry Schwabsky *Heretics of Language*
Barry Schwabsky *Trembling Hand Equilibrium*
Jeremy Sigler *Crackpot*
Jørn H. Sværen *Queen of England* (trans. Jørn H. Sværen)
Genya Turovskaya *The Breathing Body of This Thought*
Matvei Yankelevich *Some Worlds for Dr. Vogt*